Life is a
PARADOX

Counter-Intuitive Secrets to
Personal and Professional Effectiveness

D1002492

Al Ritter

I
FFP

Financial Forum Publishing
Logan, UT 84321
435.750.0062

Publisher's Note

This publication is designed to provide accurate and authoritative information with regard to the subject matter covered. It is sold with the understanding that the publisher is not engaged in rendering legal, accounting or other professional services. If you require legal advice or other expert assistance, you should seek the services of a competent professional.

ISBN 978-0-9786010-7-2

Printed in the United States of America
Cover Design by L Fisher

Acknowledgement

We have an old saying in the management consulting business: In a successful client engagement, we learn as much or more from our clients as they learn from us.

That seemingly paradoxical truth goes a long way in expressing my appreciation to so many people who have helped make this book possible:

- John Childs, President of J.W. Childs Associates, whose wisdom and friendship I have valued for many years.

- My valued clients, especially Ray Rudy, Jim Murphy, Bob Devine, Mario Soussou, Allan Dowds, Bruce Truman and the many others in their organizations who have been willing to face tough issues and create breakthroughs for themselves and their organizations.

- My many other clients, past and present, who have contributed so much to me personally and to this book.

- My family, especially my wife Barbara and my daughters Ashley and Andrea, who prove to me every day that the truly important things in life and work are a function of the heart.

- My long-time friends Tom Mastandrea, John Russert, Randy Roach, Jerry Stadheim, Rich Seigel, Joanie Muench, Dick Grieve, Lou Bellande, Steve Drozdeck and Jim Hallene who are always there when I need advice and encouragement.

- Old friends from high school, college, business school, and the Army, and new friends from Chicago-land and other places. I am deeply grateful for your continuing friendship and wisdom. As the years go by, my appreciation for you grows even stronger.

- My publisher, Lyn Fisher, and editor, Sheri Lear, whose insight, experience, encouragement and knowledge are greatly valued.

Table of Contents

Chapter 1: Slow Down in Order to Speed Up 1

Addressing the counter-intuitive idea that we can actually get more done and become more effective by slowing down or even ceasing our activity, this chapter examines some interesting paradoxes that reflect the reality of today's world, such as having more conveniences but less time, or having less time to think before responding. The reader will learn ways to counter these modern tendencies by consciously slowing down.

Chapter 2: The Gift of Listening 7

This chapter demonstrates the paradoxical notion that listening is more important than speaking. Conscious and intentional listening can, in fact, be the greatest gift we can offer another person. We will learn why listening, not speaking, is the foundation of great leadership, high performance teams, and effective organizations.

Chapter 3: Angels in Disguise 13

Here we explore the paradoxical notion that those people who we tend to discount because they look or act differently often turn out to be among our greatest blessings. These special people are often "angels in disguise" and can be identified by their propensity toward true goodness. I use my daughter Ashley, who has Down syndrome, as an example of someone who offers unconditional love and acceptance to all those around her. She has taught us far more than we could ever teach her. The chapter also identifies other "angels in disguise" and reminds us of the importance of rising above our human tendency to discredit people who look or act differently.

Chapter 4: The 100/0 Principle 19

The 100/0 Principle is introduced, which teaches us how to create and sustain important relationships. We learn how to take full (100%) responsibility for a relationship and expect nothing (0%) in return. The paradox is that when we accept full responsibility for the relationship, it often shifts to a 100/100 partnership, with each person taking equal — and total — responsibility. This is great news for the individuals involved. This philosophy also works for teams, organizations and families.

The culture of North America supports the adage: "look out for number one." When we do the opposite, however — focus on others rather than ourselves — a most interesting paradox occurs; not only are other people and even entire companies influenced favorably, but our own personal happiness, satisfaction and effectiveness will reach new heights. When we serve others, we profoundly serve ourselves as well.

This chapter speaks to the paradoxical notion that developmentally disabled people, such as my daughter Ashley, can be an enormous gift to their families, as well as the many others whose lives they touch. The chapter is touchingly co-authored by Ashley's sister, Andrea, who speaks of her experiences growing up with a disabled sister and the unexpected and profound impact Ashley has had on her life.

It is often the smallest things that make the biggest difference. This is as true in one's home life as it is in the workplace. The chapter discusses ten examples of this paradox, including how common courtesies create uncommon impact, the power of "speaking accomplishment," the importance of being on time, and other seemingly insignificant details.

In this chapter, we explore the paradoxical idea that breakdowns and problems, when handled well, are a primary means to accomplishing the extraordinary. This is not a chapter about positive thinking; on the contrary, handling breakdowns involves a truthful acknowledgement of the problem, a re-examination of our commitment, and a new plan of action. When handled well, breakdowns are indeed major precursors to significant breakthroughs.

In the business world, there is much talk about mission, vision and strategy. In our daily conversations, we also spend much time in the conversational domain of assessment, where we state our opinions or make complaints in ways that are unproductive. In reality, talk is often insignificant. What's not obvious to many people is that words are of little value unless we translate them into decisive, coordinated action. This chapter helps readers develop skills in the domain of action, to allow them to produce true breakthroughs in productivity and results. The results we produce are a function of the actions we take.

Most people don't understand the profound effect conversations have on our lives. In this chapter, we explore three types of speaking: straight talk, alignment and acknowledgment, and find out how these communication styles help teams and organizations reach peak performance.

In this concluding chapter, the "three domain" model is presented in order to pull together the important principles of the earlier chapters. The model consists of three domains: past, present and future. We explain why our actions are best guided by future influences, such as commitment, vision or goals rather than by past influences, including former assessments, judgments or assumptions.

The final section includes exercises to help the reader incorporate the strategies learned in this book into their personal and professional lives.

Introduction

*L**ife is a Paradox*** demonstrates that the most important lessons in life and work are often paradoxical — that is, they are not readily apparent and often conflict with our expectations.

The impetus for this book comes from my 20 years of experience as a management consultant to thousands of people, teams and organizations worldwide. The book also owes its genesis to my experiences as a father to my daughter Ashley, who has Down syndrome. The chapter about Ashley is co-authored with my other daughter, Andrea, who speaks to the paradoxical notion that a developmentally disabled person like Ashley can be — and, in fact, has been — a great gift to our family and the countless others whose lives have been touched by her.

Many of life's other important lessons are similarly counter-intuitive. In fact, even our *access* to personal and professional satisfaction and effectiveness is often counter-intuitive. For this reason, most people need help navigating that path. Through the use of many examples from my personal life, the workplace and even sports, this book will provide you with straightforward and direct access to the type of thinking and behavior that can lead to vastly improved success and satisfaction in both your personal and professional lives.

In my work I have learned that strategies that create the greatest positive change are not obvious; they are, in fact, counter-intuitive or paradoxical. This book will help you identify these strategies and use them in your relationships with family members, friends and co-workers. Truly expansive thinkers will find they can even apply the concepts in this book to societal and global issues.

This is the first book of its kind to tackle the paradoxical nature of life's most important lessons. You will begin to notice your natural tendencies toward automatic responses to situations, and learn to make conscious choices to think and act differently — paradoxically — in order to achieve enormous improvements in your relationships, productivity and personal satisfaction.

Each chapter will introduce a paradoxical notion, which will be followed up with real-life examples of how people's acceptance, acknowledgement and adoption of these principles can have profound effects on their lives.

The final section of the book includes exercises to help you practice and perfect your newfound skills.

I hope you enjoy reading this book and that it affects you and those around you positively.

✳✳✳

"How to Proceed" Tips

People often ask me to provide them with simple tips on how to effectively implement the ideas covered in our workshops and coaching sessions. These same strategies apply to the ideas in this book.

Regardless of which issue we are facing, we must determine how we typically react to a situation, and then distinguish a different, counter-intuitive response.

It looks like this:

Something happens in our life ...

• Our *typical* reaction:
  Automatic response, based on judgment or preconceived notion

  Consequence of response:
  Less than satisfactory

• An alternative, *counter-intuitive* response:
  We *catch/notice* the way in which we are about to react
  We *choose* to respond in a different way

  Consequence of response:
  Typically satisfaction and effectiveness

Thus, the two keys are AWARENESS and CHOICE. We are *aware* of our automatic tendencies, and then we *consciously choose* how we are going to respond.

For example, think about the way we tend to listen to each other, as is described in Chapter 2 — The Gift of Listening. Our automatic tendency is to listen to others in a judgmental way, which

I describe as "right/wrong" or "agree/disagree." However, we can train ourselves to be *aware* of our automatic listening, and then consciously and intentionally *choose* to listen creatively, thereby rising above our judgmental tendencies.

The overall challenge with any of the issues in this book is to determine who is in charge. Are your automatic thoughts in charge of your responses, or are *you* in charge of your responses? We have a choice. Our effectiveness is based on our ability to be in charge — to take personal responsibility for our responses to situations.

As you read this book, remember to keep these two keys in mind: *Awareness* and *Choice.*

> "Few people think more than two or three times
> a year; I have made an international reputation
> for myself by thinking once or twice a week."
>
> —— George Bernard Shaw

Chapter

Slow Down
In Order To Speed Up

Aparadox is a concept that seems absurd or contradictory, yet is true. The idea of slowing down in order to speed up is certainly paradoxical. It simply conflicts with our sense of logic. Yet it is one of the most important lessons to be learned in life and in business. When we consciously slow down, or even temporarily cease activity, our productivity actually increases.

John Wooden, the renowned former basketball coach at UCLA, had a favorite saying: "Be quick, but don't be in a hurry." After meeting Coach Wooden, attending some of his practices and games, and reading some of his books, I think I have a better idea of what he meant. It seems to me that his statement refers to committing to certain behaviors and avoiding others. Be prepared ... be alert ... be efficient *but* don't rush ... don't be careless ... don't take things for granted.

If you consider the realities of our current lifestyle in America, you'll note that we have a long way to go to adhere to Coach Wooden's advice.

Consider the following.

We tend to:
- Have more conveniences, but less time
- Have short tempers and narrow viewpoints
- Listen too little, talk too much
- Drive too fast
- Get too little sleep
- Eat too much, too fast
- Spend more time at work, less time with loved ones
- Think with our head, not with our heart
- React, rather than reflect and think

One antidote to this hurried lifestyle is to take time to pause and think before deciding our next move.

Stopping

One of the most profound ways to speed up productivity is to simply stop activity. These periods of cessation can range from a few brief moments to several months. Below are some short-term, medium-term and long-term suggestions for ceasing activity:

Short term:
- After a phone call, pause for 10 seconds to think about what to do next
- Before an important meeting, pray for God's

guidance and wisdom
- Take the time to say thanks for a favor
- Say "I love you," or give a kiss or hug to your partner and loved ones

Medium term:
- Take a walk
- Eat lunch somewhere other than your desk
- Brainstorm ideas — even wild and crazy ones — with co-workers
- Turn off the TV and read a book
- Start your day with yoga, meditation and/or prayer

Long term:
- Take a vacation without access to phone or e-mail
- Take a several month-long sabbatical without an agenda

When talking about the sources of his great ideas, Albert Einstein said, "I lived in solitude in the country and noticed how the monotony of quiet life stimulates the creative mind." In fact, many researchers in the field of creativity believe that insight occurs during the reflection and relaxation that follows a period of intense activity and work. Today our minds are rarely silent; we need to give ourselves the gift of reflection and relaxation.

Some U.S. firms are beginning to see the benefits of downtime. For example, many companies shut down their operations between Christmas and New Year's, giving virtually all of their employees time off with pay. Needless to say, employees react quite favorably to this compensated time off, appreciating the forced break from e-mails, phone calls or other work-related activities. Some employers even go a step further, rewarding those who use their allotted vacation time with better performance reviews and/or higher pay. One Chicago hotel offers to help electronic device-addicted vacationers relax by locking up their cell phones and laptops during their stay.

The United States may be the only industrialized nation with no mandated national holidays or vacation period that private employers are obligated to recognize. On top of that, Americans get fewer paid days off — an average of 10-15 days per year — than any other industrialized nation. For example, the French and Austrians have six weeks or more each year.

Experts say vacation neglect has consequences. Overworked employees are more likely to make mistakes and resent their bosses and co-workers. Studies have also revealed that these people have more health issues than their rejuvenated counterparts.

Without exception, my clients who have implemented cessations into their routines have reported increased levels of effectiveness, productivity and personal satisfaction significantly beyond their expectations.

Walking Fast

It seems that we are in a perpetual hurry, reinforced by a culture that constantly generates new innovations aimed at speeding things along. Fast food enables us to eat a meal without sitting at a table, let alone getting out of the car. E-mail and fax machines have made regular mail all but obsolete. Cell phones allow us to conduct business on a bus, train, or even the dinner table. A number of states, such as Illinois, have the I-Pass, which allows drivers to speed through the tollbooth without taking the time to personally pay the attendant. Furthermore, it seems that we have become so accustomed to the fast pace that we can no longer handle delays (think of "road rage").

My friend Andy tells the story of a woman who entered a long-distance walking race from Seattle to Miami. She was enjoying a leading spot in the race when she came to an important realization. Her goal was not to finish first. In fact, her goal was not necessarily to finish at all. Her true goal, she realized, was to establish relationships along the way. As described in the Biblical parable of the vine and the branches in John 15:1-17, she discovered that we are all connected and we need one another. What matters most are the people we meet on the way to wherever we're going, whether on a cross-country walking journey or a life journey. We need to slow down our pace, perhaps even come to a complete stop, in order for this to happen.

Saying No

Another example of slowing down in order to speed up is learning to remain focused on one task at a time. This often means saying no to demands outside your area of focus. This includes unforeseen demands, such as unproductive meetings that often result in over-commitment. In order to do this, you must be aware of the human propensity to do many things in a mediocre manner, rather than doing a few things very well.

Eliminating Distractions

Checking e-mail and voicemails can become addictive. I suggest devoting one time slot each day to respond to e-mails and phone calls. Don't hesitate to close your office door and let your phone calls go to voicemail to deter interruptions. You're much more likely to finish a project on time if you focus all your attention on the task.

The key to making this concept work is to make a conscious choice to include some ways to pause or stop activity into your routine. By recognizing and adopting the paradoxical notion that a slow down can actually result in a speed up, we can achieve an unprecedented level of effectiveness and satisfaction in both our work and personal lives.

✳✳✳

Chapter 1. Key Point to Remember

Observe the many characteristics of our times that push you to react, rather than reflect and think. Then consciously choose to slow down or, even temporarily, stop what you are doing.

" Everyone should be quick to listen,
and slow to speak and slow to anger."

— James 1:19

Chapter

The Gift of Listening

In our teambuilding workshops, we teach that listening
is often the greatest gift we can offer another person.
Participants in our workshops are typically skeptical about
this concept — and why shouldn't they be? Our culture clearly
emphasizes speaking over listening and, whether we like it or
not, we are all influenced by our culture.

However, in our consulting work we have learned that listening
is the most direct and powerful means to creating relationships.
We have also discovered that listening is the foundation for great
leadership, high-performance teams, and effective organizations.

When we listen effectively to another, we are not only giving that person a great gift, but we also are giving ourselves a great gift as well. Life is a paradox in many ways, and this is one of them. Let's examine this a little more closely.

Automatic Listening

It is useful to identify the way in which most people usually listen. We have labeled this "automatic" listening and it takes two forms: Not listening at all, or listening through a set of filters of which we aren't even fully aware. The most prevalent filters through which we listen are right/wrong or agree/disagree; in other words, our listening is often judgmental in nature, based on our preconceived notions or past conclusions and reactions. And to make matters worse, we tend to be quick to judge others negatively, either by making them wrong or being quick to see the areas of disagreement we have with them. We often don't give people much of a chance.

While listening through the right/wrong filter is the most prevalent manner of automatic listening, there are others as well. Do you recognize any of these?

- Looking for the fatal flaw
- Thinking about what we're going to say when we have a chance to talk
- Concluding that there is no validity to what's being said
- Assuming we already know this information
- Looking for the bottom line
- Trying to figure out how the information fits in with what we already know

Creative Listening

As a listener, it is important to determine who is in charge — your automatic thoughts and responses, or you. Either the conversations have you or you have the conversations. And you have a choice.

The first key to changing our listening habits is to take notice of our automatic listening. Perhaps we can do this by giving ourselves a mental reminder (example: "Here I go again"). We can then make the choice to listen differently — to consciously and intentionally implement what we call "creative listening." When we engage in creative listening, we intentionally listen for a number of things such as:

- What is the speaker's commitment?
- What are the possibilities here?
- What can I learn?
- What is the speaker's reality?
- What are the speaker's concerns?
- Where can we align?
- What would work?

When we choose to listen creatively, we give people a real chance to be heard. We also offer our teams and organizations the chance to have true collaboration, communication, creativity, risk-taking and trust.

Sailing Across the Pacific

Veteran movie actor Hal Holbrook tells the story of his solo voyage across the Pacific Ocean on his 40-foot sailboat some years ago. He recalls how his elbow repeatedly bumped against every sharp corner of the boat. Each time it happened, he instinctively looked around for somebody to blame, even though he was alone!

People go to great lengths to avoid being at fault. Even a solo sailor operated out of the human tendency to blame someone else. Mr. Holbrook demonstrated the typical right/wrong automatic listening, even though the voice he was listening to was his own!

Coaching a Senior Leader

During a recent consulting engagement, a member of the company's senior leadership team asked if I could sit with her and coach her on a problem she was having. I agreed, and we met for an hour.

During the time we were together, I really listened to her concerns. Rather than offering advice, I simply acknowledged her concerns with an occasional "Uh-huh" or "I understand." I did a great deal of listening and very little talking. At the end of the hour she had reached a clear resolution to her problem. "That was the best conversation I've had in a long time," she told me. "I can't thank you enough."

All I did was listen.

Meeting My Son

Our workshops almost always include a section on Listening. We give the participants a homework assignment. We ask them to have a conversation with a family member or friend, take notice of their own automatic listening, and then consciously choose to listen creatively. The next morning we ask our participants to report on what happened when they altered their listening pattern. One participant relayed the following: "My son came home from school with a problem last night. I just listened. He figured it out for himself and then said 'Thanks, Dad.' By simply listening to him creatively, I sensed that I met my son for the first time. He is 16 years old."

Have a conversation with a family member or friend, take notice of your automatic listening, and then consciously choose to listen creatively.

Effective Selling

My friend Will sells software systems to the healthcare industry. He wins all kinds of sales awards. Of course, I asked him how he does it. "It's simple," he explained. "When I meet with a prospect, I do almost no talking and a lot of listening. More specifically, the little talking I do involves asking questions about their business and its challenges. All the rest is listening."

Learning from "Unlikely" Sources

Before becoming a consultant, I spent 18 years in corporate positions. During that time I had the privilege of working with Joe Sullivan, CEO of Swift & Company. Once or twice a year we went to a planning session at an off-site location for a couple of days. Invariably, Joe would disappear shortly after we arrived at the hotel or conference center. But we always knew where to find him — he would be in a remote section of the facility talking with the janitor, security guard, or another behind-the-scenes person.

We asked Joe why he did this. "Oh, that's simple," he would say. "I like to ask questions and listen to those folks; they always teach me something. They often have a unique perspective on things — I learn a lot from them."

A Lesson from Eisenhower

I recently read some stories about Dwight Eisenhower during his tenure as Commander of Allied Forces in World War II. I learned an important lesson from him. Eisenhower had a penchant for mingling with the troops informally, often beginning conversations with, "What do you think about … ?" That's a lesson worth remembering.

A Lesson from Effective CEOs and Other Leaders

In more than 20 years of management consulting, I have found that the most effective leaders share this trait: They routinely get out of their offices and learn from people at all levels of their organizations. They inquire as to their thoughts about the company's strengths and weaknesses and ideas for changes. The conversation primarily consists of the leader asking questions and then really listening to the responses.

When things aren't working in your organization, when there is little cooperation and communication, the chances are someone (very often you) is trying to be right rather than finding out what works. I believe this has cost most of us at least one important relationship, and that cost is too high!

Listening grants others the power of speaking. We're really talking about creating effective communication between people, functions and organizations. The greatest gift you can give another is the gift of listening. Even someone who speaks poorly under adverse circumstances can be better understood when we are willing to listen creatively. We can choose to do this at any time under any circumstances.

The Four Principles of Listening:
- Listening grants others the power of speaking.
- Listening is a gift. We are often not generous with this gift.
- Perhaps what we have to *listen* to is more important than what we have to say.
- Communication is what is heard, not what is said.

❊❊❊

Chapter 2: Key Point to Remember

Notice your tendency to "listen automatically" to another, especially judgmentally, and deliberately choose to create a new, more generous listening to that person.

"We don't see things as *they* are.
We see things as *we* are"

— Anais Nin

Chapter

Angels in Disguise

It is human tendency to discredit, judge or even fear people who look or act differently than us. We are more often drawn to those who are similar to us in some way — ethnicity, religion, culture, even temperament. Yet one of the important lessons I have learned is that often, hidden within some of those people we judge or disregard, is an angel in disguise. I'm sure you have met at least one of these angels. They demonstrate pure goodness through their actions, often unexpectedly and in unlikely situations.

In this chapter I'll tell you about some of the angels I have encountered in my life and teach you the importance of looking beyond the superficial layers of a person you might otherwise discount to discover the angel within.

A Gift Called Ashley

When our daughter Ashley was born in 1980, my wife Barbara and I were devastated to learn she had Down syndrome. We were heartbroken. We knew our lives would be significantly altered from that day forward. We feared that our lives would be completely ruined.

Ashley is now a grown woman. In some ways our worst fears came true — she has an IQ of only 36, speaks very little and can't perform even simple tasks without extensive prompting. But, in other (more important) ways, Ashley has been an angel in disguise. She is gentle, full of love and unconditionally accepting of others. Her spirit rubs off on others, including my wife Barbara, our other daughter Andrea (see chapter six), and me. In fact, we often say that Ashley teaches us a great deal more than we teach her.

Ashley softens our hearts. In 2002, we placed her at Mount St. Joseph, a residential facility in Lake Zurich, Illinois. About a month after she moved there we were called to a parent-staff conference. As we walked in the room one of the staff said "You two must be very proud of Ashley." We assured her that we were, and asked what prompted that comment. "Oh, it's a wonderful thing to see," she replied. "Ashley has such a sweet and giving spirit, and she has already positively influenced many of the other residents. We are so glad she is here with us."

Is that music to a parent's ears or what? What parent wouldn't want to hear words like that spoken about their child?

A friend of mine recently noted that Ashley doesn't let her head get in the way of her heart. She has been the prime catalyst in my life to help me achieve a healthier head/heart balance. She consistently practices taking full responsibility for the relationship and expecting nothing in return. (See the 100/0 Principle in Chapter 4.) Ashley is a true angel in disguise for me and for many others!

The Homeless in New York City

In the 1970s, Barbara and I lived in an area called Tudor City, located near the United Nations plaza in New York City. In those days I played a lot of basketball on the outdoor court at the corner of 40th Street and FDR Drive.

Often there were several homeless people hanging around the court. At first I didn't pay attention to them; in fact, I hoped they would go away. I was afraid of them. I found them unappealing. They didn't leave, so over several weeks I started interacting with them. Their leader was a guy named "Irish."

As I got to know them, Irish and his friends shattered my image of the homeless. They may have been filthy on the outside, but they were pure of heart on the inside. They remain among the nicest, most considerate people I have ever known. Talking and shooting baskets with Irish and his pals became a highlight of my days.

What particularly impressed me was the exemplary team they formed. They were "all for one and one for all." Their fundamental commitment was to take care of each other — to literally help each other survive. Irish and his friends demonstrated many characteristics of high-performance teams that years later became cornerstones of my consulting practice:

- Willingness to take a stand (in their case, for each other's survival)
- Penchant for straight talk (being open and honest)
- Ability to align with each other (fully support a decision), even in the face of dissention
- Ability to handle problems without being defeated

Their commitment to each other was beautiful to behold, and a great learning experience for me.

A Nurse's Legacy

My mother was a registered nurse. As a child I frequently met another nurse or a doctor who would sing her praises. However, her inner angel didn't become fully apparent to me until I was 23 and a company commander in the U.S. Army in Kaiserslautern, Germany.

Our company's mission was to haul refrigerated cargo throughout Western Europe. We had kids, ages 18 to 20 years old, driving the large tractor-trailer rigs. One of our drivers, Dave King, had a terrible accident. His tractor was a crumpled mess, and he nearly died.

My parents happened to be visiting me at the time of King's accident. I invited them to accompany me to the hospital to see Dave. What a sight he was — covered from head to toe with bandages, small slits for his eyes, nose and mouth. The doctor whispered to us that Dave's injuries were so severe that his survival was unlikely.

We all spoke some words of encouragement and comfort to Dave. He could only respond with grunts and moans. Then an amazing thing happened. My mom pulled up a chair right next to Dave. She spoke to him in a hushed tone for an hour!

Several months later, as Dave was on his way to a full recovery, he wrote my mom a letter. It said in part: "You know better than anyone that I was about to give up in those first days after the accident. I was in pain. I had lost all hope of surviving. Then you came along. You told me you had seen people survive who were in worse shape than me. You said life was too precious to give up. You restored my hope and my will to live. I am sure I am alive today because of you. How can I ever thank you?"

For Dave King, my mom was an angel in disguise.

Living Happily to 100 and Beyond

I have read some compelling research studies about Blue Zones — regions of the world where people live longer than anywhere else, often to 100 and beyond. These Blue Zones include such places as Okinawa, Japan; Sardinia, Italy; Loma Linda, California; and Nicoya Peninsula, Costa Rica. Researchers studying these areas have pinpointed some common lifestyle characteristics among those living in Blue Zones that could contribute to their longevity. Among the factors is a strong support network, not only of friends, neighbors and family members, but also of visitors (strangers) who they routinely welcome into their communities and lives. The centenarians in the world's Blue Zones refer to those in their social network as angels from God. You and I might recognize them as "angels in disguise."

A Great Leader

In a previous chapter I spoke about a man I greatly respect — my former boss, Joe Sullivan, who was president of Swift and Company in the 1980s. One of the things that made him an effective leader was his ability to seek out and recognize the angels in disguise.

You will recall that Joe would often disappear when we were away on a "boondoggle" at a fancy hotel or resort. We discovered that he was spending his free time with the hotel's support staff, having long discussions about everything from the facility's operations to world events. Why did he do this? According to Joe, these were "real people" who saw the world more clearly than most of us. They were honest. He learned a great deal from their insights.

Joe used these experiences to implement a successful strategy at Swift called the "front-line management system," in which decision making was pushed down to the lowest possible levels. He was confident it would work. He truly believed that those in the "front line" of any organization had more knowledge and ability than most people gave them credit for. They were, in essence, the angels in disguise of the organization.

You probably can guess the rest of the story: In three years, Swift progressed from a break-even operation to the top third of the entire food industry in all meaningful profitability measures.

Joe Sullivan and others like him don't fall into the trap of allowing human nature to prematurely discredit the value of another person. They make a concerted effort to rise above that all-too-common reaction.

The angels in our lives can teach us important lessons. We would be wise to be slow to judge others and make assumptions about the people in our lives, because angels come in all kinds of disguises. Regardless of the first impressions we have of others, we need to give them a real chance with us. We need to be alert for "angels in disguise."

Chapter 3: Key Point to Remember

Always remind yourself that "angels" come in all sizes, shapes and colors. So interact with others with graciousness and acceptance, and you will give yourself a chance to receive a true blessing from an "angel in disguise."

> "True discovery consists not in finding new landscapes,
> but in seeing the same landscape with new eyes."
>
> —— Marcel Proust

Chapter

The 100/0 Principle

Most of us are familiar with the notion that a good relationship is based on a 50/50 proposition. It goes something like this, "I'll do my 50%, you do your 50%, and we'll have a great relationship." Of course, the problem is that when something breaks down in the relationship, each person tends to blame the other — to point the finger as if it were their fault.

A few years ago a philosopher came up with a new relationship theory — the 100/100 proposition. It goes like this, "I'll take 100% responsibility, you do the same, and we can't miss." This looked good at first; however, in practice it had the same shortcoming as did the 50/50 proposition, namely each person playing the blame game. The 100/100 idea has another inherent flaw. Each person has high, even unrealistic expectations, of the other.

After all, each person expects the other to take full responsibility.

So what does it take to create and sustain great relationships with others? It's the 100/0 principle: "I take full responsibility for the relationship (the 100%), expecting nothing in return (the 0%)." This may strike you as strange; but, here's the paradox: When I take authentic responsibility for a relationship with another, more often than not the other person quickly chooses to take responsibility for the relationship also. Consequently, the 100/0 relationship transforms to something approaching 100/100. When that occurs, true breakthroughs happen for the individuals involved, their teams, their organizations and their families.

Tips for Implementing the 100/0 Principle

Implementing the 100/0 principle is not natural for most of us. It takes real commitment to the relationship and a good dose of self-discipline to think and act as follows:

Determine what you can do to make the relationship work — then do it. This usually includes your demonstration of respect and kindness to the other person, whether they deserve it or not.

Do not expect anything in return.

Do not allow anything the other person says or does, no matter how annoying, to affect you. In other words, don't take the bait.

Pre-eminent Relationships

Without fully realizing it, many of us operate out of the principle of right/wrong. We determine our relationship with others based on whether we agree or disagree with them, or whether we think they are right or wrong.

However, certain relationships in our lives are too important to operate on the right/wrong principle. In those relationships the 100/0 principle applies; whereby, one is willing to take full responsibility for the relationship with another, expecting nothing in return. Each of us must determine the relationships to which this principle should apply. For most of us it applies to family, friends, work associates and customers with whom we are obliged to interact.

Breakthrough at Work

When I was the Chief Financial Officer of a Fortune 500 consumer goods company, I reported to the company's president as well as the CFO of our parent company. I did not like the CFO, and I'm quite sure the feeling was mutual. My immediate boss (Jack, my company's president) got wind of this and one day gave me a surprising directive:

"Al, I want you to immediately create a relationship with Paul. It's your most important short-term goal and I am counting on you to do it."

"Jack," I responded, "that's the hardest thing you could ask me to do. Do you really mean it?"

"I sure do," he answered.

"You mean I should create a *business* relationship, don't you?" I inquired.

"I mean a relationship, period," Jack answered. "And if you can create a great personal relationship with Paul, all the better."

Well, I didn't like it, but the directive was crystal clear. Jack was telling me I was to be the 100% in a 100/0 relationship with Paul.

I didn't know what to do at first, but then it struck me that I should simply treat Paul with the same decency and respect with which I treated others. And even though it was uncomfortable at first, that's exactly what I did.

Guess what happened? Almost immediately, Paul began to respond to me in kind; the very behavior that initially caused me to dislike him disappeared. We went on to have a strong relationship for the two years we continued working together. The 100/0 principle served me well in a work situation where it was important for two people to work together effectively.

As a business coach, I almost always use the 100/0 principle with my clients. In a recent engagement, an investment team adopted the 100/0 principle in working with each other. As their team chemistry and rapport grew, their investment results grew commensurately.

Breaking Through the Silo

Probably the most common business application of the 100/0 principle is the tendency for people to adopt a so-called "silo" mentality. This is where one's relationships with others in the same function (or silo) are significantly stronger than their relationships with people in other functions.

In a recent consulting engagement, we worked in a mid-sized company with the senior vice president of operations and his counterpart, the senior vice president of marketing. The two leaders had a strong dislike for each other, and their relationship was filled with finger pointing and blame. After helping both leaders understand the 100/0 principle and apply it with each other, their relationship shifted to something resembling 100/100, and the measurable results of their functions and the entire company began to set all-time records. They will tell you that the single most important factor in those breakthrough results was their adoption of the 100/0 principle.

Breakthrough on the Home Front

My mom, who passed away a few years ago, was an admirable person in many ways. However, during the first few years of our marriage, my wife Barbara and I often became upset with her numerous "digs" about our lifestyle. Our upset finally triggered a confrontation with my mom and dad, and we didn't see them for a year. Fortunately, Barbara saw the error of our ways. She made me realize our relationship with my mom was more important than who was right or wrong.

I will never forget the phone call to my mom after a year of not speaking. I asked her to forgive Barbara and me, and I told her I was glad that she and dad were my parents. I told her we were fine except for missing her, and asked if we could come for a visit. As I was talking, I felt the phone line between Chicago and Florida expand to an infinite width, symbolic of our new acceptance of each other.

> "If you want to change someone, change yourself first." — Mom

Barbara and I quickly went to visit my parents. On the way there we made a pact to not let anything anyone said upset us. Although my mom made a few of her familiar "digs," we responded without anger. "You know, mom," we'd say, "we'll really think about that." Or even, "You're probably right."

Until my mom's death 10 years later, we enjoyed a truly great relationship. I had a mom again. For those 10 years, we can't recall hearing one "dig" from her — another example of the 100/0 principle leading to a 100/100 relationship.

As I was growing up, my mom often said, "If you want to change someone, change yourself first." Little did I know that her wise insight would eventually contribute so directly to my own relationship with her.

Success in Marriage

The marriage relationship may be the best example of where the 100/0 principle applies — where the relationship is more important than who is right or wrong.

I have noticed a common theme running through many successful marriages: Opposites really do attract and they seem to create marriages that work. Those marriages often seem to involve people of different backgrounds, interests and views. I believe the 100/0 principle provides some explanation for this.

Two people of similar backgrounds and interests will likely have preconceived, although usually unstated, expectations of each other; they assume a 50/50 relationship. On the other hand, two very different people will tend to realize from the very beginning that similar expectations will lead nowhere. The notion of who is right or wrong takes a distinct back seat to each partner asking "What can I do to make this relationship work?"

That's the essence of the 100/0 principle. Person A focuses on being gracious to and listening to Person B, rather than focusing on preconceived notions or expectations about Person B.

Here is an example: My friend Jerry has a son and daughter. A few years ago his son married a woman from his hometown. Meanwhile, Jerry's daughter married a man who was born and raised in a foreign country. Jerry tells me his son's marriage is heading for divorce. "They're just too much alike," he told me.

However, the good news is that his daughter's marriage is thriving. Jerry says he can't quite put his finger on it, but there seems to be a mutual respect for each other's differences. When I told Jerry about the 100/0 principle, he immediately responded, "That's it! Each takes responsibility for their relationship, with few expectations of the other."

A word of caution, there are some circumstances (thankfully, relatively few) where the 100/0 principle does not apply. Examples include situations in which the other person's behavior is intolerable, such as: lying, cheating, stealing, or committing a crime. In those circumstances, that person's behavior would likely dictate actions on your part quite different from actions stemming from the 100/0 principle.

Notwithstanding that word of caution, the 100/0 principle is the simplest, most direct and most effective way to create solid relationships. Shift your thinking from "it takes two to tango" to "I can and will create a relationship with that person." Take responsibility for the success of the relationship, expect nothing in return, and watch what happens!

Chapter 4: Key Point to Remember

Take full responsibility for your relationship with another person by consciously choosing to suspend judgment of that person and, instead, treat him or her with respect and dignity whether deserved or not.

> "Life's most persistent and urgent question is,
> 'What are you doing for others?'"
>
> —— Martin Luther King

Chapter

Put Self on Shelf

The culture in North America supports the familiar adage, "look out for number one." Mass media constantly tries to convince us that physical beauty, usually defined by a slim body and an unnaturally youthful appearance, is the key to true happiness. In being so self consumed, we often ignore the needs of others, and, paradoxically, overlook a prime source of our own happiness, satisfaction and effectiveness.

Imagine what would happen if we shifted our concern from ourselves to others. What if every time we looked in the mirror, instead of seeing minor physical flaws in need of costly repairs, we saw a true servant of others? What if we shifted from an assumption of entitlement to an assumption of servitude? The outcome would be a literal miracle — a world with unprecedented compassion. By putting one's "self on the shelf," a most interesting paradox could emerge — the achievement of a level of personal satisfaction, happiness and effectiveness far beyond what is possible by looking out for number one.

A CEO Sees the Light

I have witnessed many examples of the "self on the shelf" concept in life and in business. In my 20 years as a management consultant, I have coached many CEOs representing a wide range of companies and industries. The concept of servant leadership often comes up; that is, the notion that the most effective leaders are typically humble individuals who see their primary role as serving others, in other words, putting their self on a shelf. In my experience, when business leaders have the courage to transform their thinking and, subsequently, their behavior in these ways, breakthrough changes occur in their relationships as well as producing measurable business results.

> ... the most effective leaders are typically humble individuals who see their primary role as serving others, in other words, putting their self on a shelf.

A CEO with whom I worked was a highly ineffective manager. He verbally abused senior executives to the point where several had quit and others were in a constant state of upset. Not surprisingly, these relationship issues had a negative impact on business, putting the entire company at risk of collapse.

With coaching, this CEO learned to shift from a micromanager with a results-at-all-costs posture to a leader committed to building powerful relationships with the people around him. He became as interested in the success of the people he managed as in his own success. As a result, he enjoys a newfound level of trust with those he manages, and his company's bottom line has set new records.

A Lesson from the Slums

A prime example of putting one's "self on the shelf" is the story of David Neeleman, the former CEO of JetBlue Airways. When David was about 20 years old, he participated in a church mission trip to serve the poor in an underprivileged area of Brazil. He was surprised by how happy he felt during his stay. He came to realize that his primary contentment came from serving others, essentially diverting attention away from himself.

Neeleman's Brazil experience is reflected in JetBlue's down-to-earth, egalitarian atmosphere, in which caring, respecting and understanding others are built into the company's culture. JetBlue was one of the few airlines that made a profit during the difficulties in the airline industry following September 11, 2001.

Watch the Spin

Our consulting firm conducts workshops for business teams. We often demonstrate the "self on the shelf" principle with a simple game of catch. We ask for a volunteer who is not skilled at catching a ball. The person typically fumbles the ball and feels a bit embarrassed.

We then change the game by asking the person to tell us which way the ball is spinning as we throw it to them. Can you guess what happens? The person begins to catch every ball, with nary a fumble. Why? The person's attention is now diverted to the ball, rather than himself or herself. When we put our self on a shelf and focus on the *other*, we can produce extraordinary results.

Don't Count Your Points

I am ashamed to admit that during my years playing high school basketball, I did a poor job of putting my "self on a shelf." Each game I kept a mental tally of the points I scored. At the end of the game my mental point count was always within one or two points of my official point total. Clearly my focus was on myself; I wanted to score a lot of points in order to look good. In retrospect, I would have been a far more valuable player had I been team-focused, helping each of my teammates achieve their potential. I learned this lesson in college from basketball great Bill Bradley.

At the University of Connecticut, we played against Bradley and his Princeton team in the NCAA Eastern Regional semi-finals. Bradley was a man among boys. At that time he was the most dominant college basketball player in the entire country. After the game we had the opportunity to speak with him. We asked him what he thought about during a game and how he was able to remain calm in the face of our verbal taunts and aggressive defense. Bradley's answer was quite revealing. He explained that he focused on his four teammates on the court. As he saw it, his job was to create a flow that would ensure maximum effectiveness for the team. By switching his focus from *self* to *team*, he greatly improved his team's performance. By the way, we won that game 52 to 50; but, in hindsight, the greatest victory was the important lesson learned.

The Annual Leadership Award

I recently spoke with Dennis Piron, the track coach of Batavia High School in Illinois. He told me about the Carolyn Regan Award, a leadership award bestowed upon worthy students at his school. The award is named in honor of one of his former athletes who graduated in 2006. He was quick to point out that this is not an annual award. It is merit based and must truly be *earned*. Dennis then told me about Carolyn.

Carolyn wasn't the best athlete, but during her four years of high school she was the glue that held the team together. She provided the chemistry. In Carolyn's senior year, two freshmen hurdlers joined the team. It was evident that these two newcomers had great potential. Carolyn immediately took them under her wing and coached them to the point where they actually surpassed her as the top hurdler. She was the consummate team-mate, demonstrating selflessness in both her actions and words. She modeled a quiet confidence that clearly permeated the entire team. She was a sister, mother and friend to everyone. Most impressive, as committed as she was to the sport, was the way she maintained a healthy life perspective by also fulfilling her commitments to academics, job, family and faith. Carolyn was a vivid example of putting oneself on the shelf.

According to Dennis, Carolyn made him a better person and coach. Hearing her story, I can understand why the Carolyn Regan Award is not bestowed on a student routinely. After all, Carolyn was not your routine student athlete.

Supreme Grace

The movie, The Passion of the Christ, depicts Jesus' final hours before he was crucified. Jesus teaches a great lesson about servitude and putting one's "self on the shelf." In the midst of unimaginable suffering, Jesus begs, "Father, forgive them, for they know not what they do." He asks his mother Mary to take care of John, "He is now your son." He prays for his disciples in those last hours, and even speaks words of comfort to one of the other men about to be executed. Regardless of one's religious persuasion, I'm sure we can all agree that Jesus was a most powerful example of putting one's "self on the shelf" regardless of the circumstances.

In a nutshell, good news abounds when we put our "self on the shelf." Those around us are influenced favorably, and we open ourselves up to an unprecedented level of personal happiness and effectiveness. When we serve others, we profoundly serve ourselves as well.

Chapter 5: Key Point to Remember

Be aware of the human tendency to think about yourself before others, and consciously shift that tendency by serving others before serving yourself.

> "Contentment is not the fulfillment of what you want,
> but the realization of what you already have."
>
> — Anonymous

Chapter

Ashley is a Blessing

In Chapter 3, I introduced you to my oldest daughter Ashley, who I referred to as an "angel in disguise." You will recall that Ashley has Down syndrome. While she has always been physically healthy, she has an I.Q. of only 36 and very limited speech. She requires much prompting to do things on her own. I will admit that my emotional state upon her birth in 1980 was one of despair; however, in the ensuing years that despair has been replaced with hope, enlightenment and love.

My daughter Andrea is three years younger than Ashley. If you ask Andrea to describe the essence of who she is, she will certainly tell you the ways in which her identity has been shaped by her sister. Through her sister, Andrea has learned the importance of unconditional love and the joy and fulfillment that comes from serving others. It is largely because of Ashley that Andrea is now a Special Education teacher in Aurora, Illinois. I want to share with you an excerpt of an essay that Andrea recently wrote about her sister:

When I was a teenager, my parents, Ashley and I attended annual family retreats at a resort in Delavan, Wisconsin. The main purpose of these retreats was to provide support for parents and siblings affected by disability. Young adult volunteers took care of the people with disabilities in order to give the families a week of reflection and peace. I participated in recreational activities as well as discussion groups with other non-disabled siblings, all of whom had brothers or sisters with some form of a physical or mental impairment.

During one discussion group, the leader asked us to state, in one word, the experience of having to care for a sibling with a disability. I am a person who often takes a while to process my thoughts, and I remember being the last one to share. Before I shared, I heard heavy words coming out of the mouths of other people in the group. Many siblings responded with the word "why," and others responded with such words as "hard," "difficult," "burdensome," and "time-consuming." Upon hearing these words I felt a pain in my heart. Even though it is often difficult for me to care for Ashley, as it's required that her needs be placed above my own, I felt that our disabled siblings deserved more understanding and grace.

When it was my turn to share, I almost blindly came out with the word "blessing." I felt compelled to share that word, not really knowing the reasons behind why I shared it. Hoping that the leader of our group would not ask me to explain, I began to shake when I heard the very question come out of her mouth, "So Andrea, why is your sister a blessing to you?"

In attempting to discover why I used the word "blessing," I remember thinking how my parents often said to me, "Andrea, do not ever tell me again that you won't take Ashley to the super-

market. That's ridiculous. Ashley deserves just as much as you to be a part of everything. She is your sister — never forget that."

During my middle school years Ashley was a sheer embarrassment. I was afraid of her awkward walk and was sure she was bothering people due to the loud bellowing noises she sometimes made. I feared my friends didn't want to be around me because of Ashley. At this time it was also hard to realize and accept that the world didn't revolve around me and my own desires.

Despite these fears and annoyances, I knew that Ashley gave me a special inner strength. I believe this inner strength stemmed from the fact that my parents were always so inclusive of Ashley in every activity. My father would walk Ashley up to big, long slides at parks, or give a lifeguard at a pool a "serious talk" if he or she would not allow Ashley to jump off the diving board. If we were to play a game such as miniature golf, Ashley would always be a part of the game. My father would always find a role for Ashley. During miniature golf he would allow Ashley to hold all the balls and instruct her to pick them up after our attempt to make a hole in one.

One aspect of my parent's consistent inclusiveness of Ashley was their attitude. They looked at Ashley's participation as a joyful experience, one that was always rewarding, even if she did something embarrassing. My father had such a love and appreciation of Ashley that I felt ashamed to voice my embarrassment of her. However, when I would voice this to him, he would respond with a comment like, "Remember that Ashley's a special kid. She helps the other kids get along with each other better. She also gives the kids an opportunity to help her out a little. She gives lots of other people the gift of love and acceptance."

My mother and father allowed me to see Ashley as a gift to those around her. Because of their guidance, gradually I was able to see Ashley as a person that deserved admiration. I have journeyed from a time in my life when I was only able to view Ashley as a burden, to the present time where I am able to walk with her into a restaurant or supermarket in a spirit of pride and hope. I am honored to say that I am very proud of who Ashley is and what she has taught me.

Ashley has allowed me to receive many gifts. My father and I often talk about how Ashley is a "master of paradox." She, as well as many other people with disabilities, often have more to teach the non-disabled population than vice versa. Ashley has given me the gifts of humility, non-judgment, gentleness and service. Ashley's disability never allows her to design her own superficial mask – she is always meek and gentle. Because of who she is, she gives other people the opportunity to know themselves more intimately. Ashley is not capable of criticism or harm; she has taught my parents and me the importance of seeking to understand before judging too quickly. Because Ashley is dependent upon our love, my parents and I must demonstrate strength in unity to gently care for her needs. She is the glue that holds my family together and the sail that keeps us pressing forward in a spirit of togetherness, openness and warmth.

In answer to the question, "So Andrea, why is your sister a blessing to you?" I said in a spirit of confidence, "Because she has taught me more than I can teach her."

The theme of this book is that the aspects of life that seem dizzying, illogical, frustrating or painful are often the ones that teach the greatest lessons. The willingness to embrace paradox is a great lesson in itself. It gives each and every person the openness and ability to seek the greater truth through the haziness of doubt and unhappiness. Having Ashley for a sister is indeed a paradox as it has enabled me to re-establish my own sense of happiness when I am around her. Since Ashley cannot carry on a conversation with me, I define my happiest moments with Ashley when she is able to repeat my name and give me one of her winning smiles. The paradox of having Ashley as a part of my family is that she has taught me to value, with gratitude, the most simple yet profound aspects of life. In this, I am able to find lasting joy.

Allow me to comment further on some of the themes in Andrea's essay:

From Despair to Hope

When Ashley was born on December 30, 1980, I was one proud father — for about an hour. That was when the doctor who delivered her walked up to me and said "Al, I think we have a problem here; I think Ashley has Down syndrome." In that moment I went from the height of ecstasy to the depth of despair — the only time in my life I've experienced anything like that. I thought our lives had been essentially ruined.

Over the next few days, weeks and months, my wife Barbara and I received wise counsel from many nurses at Central DuPage Hospital in Illinois, and visits to our home by several parents of children with Down syndrome. They assured us that our despair, while understandable, was probably unwarranted. They encouraged us to shift our outlook from despair to hope. And, with the support of these wonderful people, that's exactly what we did.

From Hope to Enlightenment and Love

As Ashley grew older we noticed that, although learning was a challenge for her, she was an unlikely but surprisingly good teacher. We all know that we can learn a great deal from our children, but the paradox here is the notion that even children with disabilities, like Ashley, can teach us a great deal too. For example, I'm naturally impatient. I like to move fast to get things done. Ashley, on the other hand, is all about being in the moment, enjoying herself and others — "smelling the roses" as it were. Observing Ashley makes me more conscious of my frenetic pace. She has taught me to monitor my behavior, exercise patience and exhibit greater tolerance.

Ashley seldom demonstrates frustration or anger when the going gets tough. She maintains a calm demeanor at all times. I remember spending a day at Wrigley Field watching the Chicago Cubs in 34-degree weather. It seemed that every kid in the ballpark, except Ashley, was complaining. Every once in a while I've kept her up until 1 or 2 a.m. Once again, never a complaint even though she was visibly tired. Our family has taken a few trips that required 10-hour car rides. You can probably guess Ashley's response — plenty of smiles, but no complaints. Her demeanor rubs off on those around her. She reminds us to enjoy each moment.

"Being" versus "Doing"

You may have heard of the philosophical distinction between being and doing.

"Doing" is what is observable, such as walking, talking, exercising, working, etc. "Being" is less tangible, such as being kind, being courteous, being happy, etc.

Ashley is almost entirely a being person. She maintains calm in the face of adversity, is kind and gracious to those she meets, and remains content regardless of the circumstances. She is a trooper when the going gets tough and is completely non-judgmental in her assessment of others. She's a good sport when things don't go her way and she is even alert and attentive in church! Overall, she serves as a role model to all of us.

This is one of the reasons that we have come to recognize Ashley as a blessing. We appreciate that she is a "being" person, not a "doing" person. In part, she is a being person out of necessity. Doing is difficult for her. She lacks the ability to do even routine tasks without encouragement and reminders. She can't do simple math. She can't talk very well. She can't easily transition from one activity to another. She can't hold eye contact for very long. Yet, we can't help but appreciate her ability to be content, to live in the moment, and to exhibit endless patience. Think of how much better the world would be if people would allow themselves the occasional luxury to just *be* rather than to constantly *do*.

Purity

Ashley's love is completely pure; it is unconditional and directly from her heart. For most of us our love wavers as real life problems arise. Ashley never seems to let life's problems interfere with her love for anyone or anything. I have come to realize that maybe, just *maybe*, Ashley is the best thing that ever happened to me.

I truly believe that if more "normal" people — those without mental or physical challenges — could overcome their fear, discomfort or reservations about people like Ashley who look or act differently, they may find that these remarkable individuals could provide them with the same kind of blessings that Ashley has given to Andrea, Barbara, me and so many others.

✳✳✳

Chapter 6: Key Point to Remember

Remember Ashley's big heart and adopt her heart-driven behavior in your own behavior. You will soon be treating all people with more kindness, including people with disabilities, and all those who look or act differently.

> "We are what we repeatedly do."
>
> — Aristotle

Chapter

The Little Stuff *is* the Big Stuff

A famous saying warns us not to "sweat the small stuff." I believe differently. The more I think about it the more I see that it is actually the "small stuff" that makes the biggest difference, both in business and in life. It's an interesting paradox. Here are 10 examples:

1. Say "Thank You"

There is no question about it, common courtesies create impact disproportionate to their simplicity. I'm certain you can think of a time when a simple "thank you" from the right person at the right time made a big difference in your life. In our workshops and seminars, we are often struck by ways in which an act of appreciation or recognition can change the course of events. I'm not exaggerating when I say that we have even observed entire corporate cultures shift when authentic acknowledgment became part of the fabric of the organization.

2. Speak Accomplishment

When I talk about "speaking accomplishment," I am referring to the act of looking for progress, as opposed to our natural tendency to only look for the end results. Speaking accomplishment is something we must consciously do.

> It is imperative for any learning organization, as it balances out the focus on results, to focus on what is learned and achieved along the way.

To begin thinking in terms of achievement rather than end results, practice acknowledging accomplishments in your own life that are more process-oriented than result-oriented:

- A difference you have made in someone's life
- A new activity you tried and enjoyed
- Something new that you learned
- A relationship that you initiated and maintained
- Something you are in the process of building: a vision, a new future, a new possibility

3. Be on Time

Whenever someone walks in late to a meeting or appointment, I am reminded of the proverbial pebble dropped in a pond:

> The immediate effect appears inconsequential; but, over time the ripples journey out in all directions.

Tardiness is typically perceived by others as disrespectful or insulting. The negative impact on teamwork, relationships and trust is not trivial. On the other hand, punctuality conveys respect for others, concern about the team and good old-fashioned courtesy. In other words, there's much more to being on time than meets the eye.

4. Create Relationships

Years ago a consulting friend told me, "Al, remember one thing: relationships are everything in business and in life." At first I was skeptical of this all-encompassing theory; but, I have now become convinced of its validity.

> Most of us, whether we admit it or not, are reluctant to initiate contact with other people, especially if they look and act different. We need to recalibrate our willingness to reach out to others — to take a chance and say something — even if it's only extending a friendly hello and a smile.

Consider the following:
- Effective salespeople know that a closed sale is contingent upon the strength of the relationship between the salesperson and the prospect. This is true whether it is a relationship that already exists or one that is in the process of being created.
- Effective employees know that creating strong relationships with co-workers at all levels is the key to individual, team and organizational performance.
- Effective leaders know that the key to their success is a dual, equal commitment to both results and *relationships*.
- Effective, happy people know that their relationships with family, friends and others are the sustenance of life and require top priority.

5. Keep Smiling

I'm not sure there's anything that has positively affected more lives than a simple smile. My dad's favorite expression is "keep smiling," and he continues to live that adage at age 95! He knows something about the power of a smile that many of us are still learning:

> A smile can be the easiest, yet most profound extension of grace, acceptance and love to another.

A smile can change a person's world. Think about that. When has someone's smile lit up your day? When has your smile lit up someone else's day? Opportunities abound for each of us to light up the world — one smile at a time.

6. Forgive Others

When we find the power to forgive, the resentment we have been harboring, sometimes for years, typically disappears. Thus:

> When we forgive others, we effectively serve ourselves.

We no longer allow our emotional lives to be controlled by others. Yet, forgiveness is sometimes a counter-intuitive, even irrational act.

Can there be any greater test of forgiveness than struggling to pardon the murder of a child? In the days after the killings of five children in a schoolhouse in Nickel Mines, Pennsylvania in 2006, the grieving Amish community taught us all a powerful lesson. They responded to the senseless murders, not with revenge, but with forgiveness, even to the point of inviting the gunman's widow to attend the funerals, and setting up funds for her three children. We all know that when it comes to forgiveness, it is easier to "talk the talk" than "walk the talk." The Amish offered all of us a superb lesson on "walking the talk."

7. Show Gratitude

Showing gratitude differs from saying "thank you" in that it is more of an internal action than an external one. Yet it is equally powerful and effective. Most of us have a great deal for which to be thankful. Sadly, most of us also spend long periods of time without thinking about this. Every day, we all need to consciously say a word or prayer of thanks.

Taking time to internally acknowledge our gratitude will, no doubt, be reflected in a sense of peace and calm that we relay to others.

8. Be Kind and Respectful to All Others

I will never forget a pop quiz given by one of my college business professors. The last question was: "What is the first name of the woman who cleans this building?" I handed in my paper, leaving the last question blank (I thought it was some kind of a joke) and, in any case, I didn't know her name. Before class ended one student asked if the last question would count toward our quiz grade. "Absolutely," said the professor. "In your careers, and in your lives, you will meet many people. All are significant. They deserve your attention and care, even if all you do is smile and say 'hello.' By the way, her name is Betty."

9. Choose to be Effective Rather than Right

Would you rather be *right* or *effective?* Keep that question front and center in your mind when you are in disagreement or conflict with someone. Don't let a knee-jerk, judgmental response sabotage your effectiveness in achieving your goals.

Effective leaders must constantly practice patience and tolerance on their way to achieving breakthrough results.

10. Be Present

Many of life's pressures cause us to divert our attention from the task at hand. We can be diverted internally by dwelling on the past, worrying about the future, or dealing with feelings of anxiety, sadness or anger. We can also be diverted by external forces, such as an interruption by a co-worker when we are trying to focus on a task or project. The goal is to maintain focus without being rude. An old saying reminds us that:

> "Nobody cares how much you know unless they know how much you care."

When someone comes into your office and you need to maintain your focus on what you're doing, look up and acknowledge them, let them know that you are not available at this moment, but set up a time to get together later.

We need to make the decision to be present, or "in the moment," in order to give our undivided attention to the opportunity before us. This will greatly improve our productivity and effectiveness, thereby reducing our stress, allowing us to ultimately live happier and healthier lives.

The little things in life truly do make a big difference. The good news is that with a little practice, virtually everyone is capable of making these seemingly little things part of their daily habits, bringing about positive results in both their personal and business lives.

※※※

Chapter 7: Key Point to Remember

Practice doing one or two of the simpler "little" things for a day, then each day gradually add more little stuff to your thinking and actions. You will be pleasantly surprised by the results.

> " For a long time, it had seemed to me that life was about to begin —
> real life. But there was always some obstacle in the way,
> something to get through first, some unfinished business,
> time still to be served, a debt to be paid. Then life would begin.
> At last, it dawned on me that these obstacles were my life.
>
> — Father Alfred D'Souza

Chapter

Breakdowns Can Produce Breakthroughs

On our journey to reach a specified goal — be it personal or professional — a setback often marks the end of the road. Setbacks, or breakdowns as I call them, are things we didn't plan for that throw us off track: an illness or injury, a broken contract, a job loss, a decline in sales or profitability … you name it. Too often when these breakdowns occur, they are met with upset, blame, resignation or avoidance of responsibility, any of which can cause an interruption or cessation of movement toward the desired goal. Teamwork, trust, creativity and action typically slow down or stop altogether.

Instead, we need to accept that life itself causes problems. Not all "bad luck" should be considered a bad thing. Someone once said, "When life gives you a kick, let it kick you forward." We need to learn to shift our view of a problem or breakdown from something bad to something that is a part of life, and when handled well, is a principal means of accomplishing the extraordinary.

> We must recognize our breakdowns in order to stop what we are doing and refocus our energies to the area that needs improvement.

Look at it this way: a breakdown can only occur if you are committed to something. The greater the commitment, the more significant the breakdown. For example, failure to win a particular case or to close a particular sale is only a breakdown if you are committed to that particular goal. No commitment, no breakdown.

Remember, something is only a breakdown if we *say* it is, if we declare it to be. We must recognize our breakdowns in order to stop what we are doing and refocus our energies to the area that needs improvement.

Now, I am not saying that we view all breakdowns as opportunities. When genuinely bad things happen, such as illness, job loss, etc., suggesting that these are opportunities is misleading and deceptive. However, we need to accept the fact that life comes with problems and that a stroke of bad luck is not always a bad thing in the end. I am suggesting that once we make the declaration and accept the reality of an unfortunate event, we can determine what actions need to be taken in order to achieve our goal. I have found time and time again that breakdowns, when handled well, often lead to extraordinary breakthroughs.

Sales Breakthrough

During one of my consulting engagements, a sales team had committed itself to a 20% increase in sales over a six-month period. After the first month, reports showed they were already falling short, and probably would not meet their goal. The team could have used these results to find blame with one another, their managers, their company or even the economy. Instead, they acknowledged the reality of the results, declared a breakdown, and went to work figuring out what went wrong. They discovered that administrative tasks were taking up time that could have been spent on sales calls. They began delegating these administrative responsibilities to others in order to spend their time in the field making calls. The result? A 26% increase in sales over a six-month period — a real breakthrough for the company!

The Lost Stories

A story was told about Ernest Hemingway in which he reportedly lost a suitcase containing most of his unpublished manuscripts. Obviously, this was a huge setback for this aspiring author. One could not blame him if he resorted to anger or despair. Fortunately, a friend and fellow author suggested that his apparent catastrophe could actually be a blessing in disguise. Hemingway returned to writing, reemerging with a more mature style. One of his first works in this newer style was the highly acclaimed book, *The Sun Also Rises*. And, as you know, he became a major figure in American literature.

An Appreciation for Life

A few years ago, I met a woman named Cheryl Wohlers who exuded such positive energy that it was hard not to notice her. As we talked she shared her story with me, including an event that occurred five years earlier and changed her life forever. She suffered serious injuries in a car accident; in fact, she narrowly escaped with her life. She had already undergone several surgeries and her doctors predicted that she would never fully recover physically. Just five years after the accident, rather than complaining about her pain and suffering, she was sharing with me the ways in which this event enhanced her life. She cited her deepened relationship with God and her new-found appreciation for life's little blessings. Her remarkable attitude in the face of adversity led me to ask her what her secret was. "As a Christian, my accident brought me closer to God," she explained. "I realized I wasn't honoring Christ fully before the accident. After the accident, I realized my life wasn't about me; it's about honoring and pleasing God rather than pleasing other people. When you're doing well, it's easy to move away from God — to put pride and self on the front burner and God on the back burner. I believe that God often uses the hardships and breakdowns in life to teach us how to appreciate Him more and to live a better life."

Despite Cheryl's ongoing struggle with her injuries, her accident enabled her to accept God fully in her life and to honor Him by the way she lives her life. What an inspiring example of a breakdown leading to a breakthrough!

Lessons from Baseball

My friend Bill Holowaty is the head baseball coach at Eastern Connecticut State University; his teams have won an unprecedented four national championships. Now Bill is a true teacher at heart, and he uses baseball as a way to teach some of life's important lessons: "Baseball mirrors life," he explains. "It teaches you that you must experience failure to achieve true success."

When a mistake is made, whether by him, one of his coaches or one of his players, he uses it as an opportunity to learn something valuable. Bill gives this example: "It's the bottom of the ninth inning. We are ahead 4-2 and playing defense. Our opponent has runners on first and second with one out. The next batter hits a long single to left center field and our centerfielder, trying to get the runner going home, overthrows the cut-off man. The run scores, the runner from first goes to third, and the batter advances to second. This puts the tying and winning runs in scoring position and eliminates the double play, giving our opponent a much easier chance to win this game."

Bill continues: "This is only a game that we can win or lose, and in life we are faced with decisions that can make a difference in the game of life every day. In life or baseball, when mistakes are made, the key question is 'what can we learn from this?'"

A mistake or setback - learn from it, and put new thinking and actions in place to prevent the same or similar mistakes from occurring in the future.

What can we learn from this? What a simple, yet profound and powerful question. What a wonderful way to look at a mistake or setback — learn from it! Put new thinking and actions in place to prevent the same or similar mistakes from occurring in the future.

The Benefits of Injury

My daughter Andrea and I participate in triathlons. We have learned that extensive training sometimes results in injuries. Injuries serve as breakdowns, or barriers, to the goal of completing a triathlon. They cause pain, interrupt training and often result in diminished overall fitness, frustration, anxiety and sometimes outright despair. But both Andrea and I have learned that good things can come from these injuries. For one thing, during the course of rehabilitation we have each learned strategies for decreasing the likelihood of subsequent injuries. We have learned to listen to our bodies, to not over-train and to rest more. We have also learned ways to make our training more efficient and effective. Perhaps most importantly, we've learned that taking time out to heal an injury is a chance to renew our commitment to our goal. We return with a renewed appreciation and revived passion for the activity, often resulting in a better performance!

When I pulled a hamstring muscle several years ago and had to miss a couple months of working out, I realized how much I loved the sport. The injury literally gave me a renewed enthusiasm and a renewed commitment to participate in triathlons.

Lessons from a Chemistry Class

A friend tells the story of his first chemistry class in high school. He was terribly intimidated by the class and afraid of making a mistake in the lab. His goal was to do well, but his trepidation was making it impossible for him to do so. A few weeks into the class, the teacher pulled him aside and explained that the very nature of the class was to experiment, make mistakes and learn from them. My friend immediately stopped trying to avoid mistakes and committed himself to actually learning the material through experimentation. The result, of course, was success; he passed the class with flying colors and learned a valuable life lesson as well.

Success is a Well-Met Series of Breakdowns

Have you ever noticed what success really looks like? Think of any accomplishment you have had, big or little, and consider what it took to get there. Rarely is any accomplishment reached via a road of continuous triumphs. In fact, almost all accomplishments in any domain of life are marked by numerous bumps in the road, and the greatest learning occurs on those detours. In other words: well-handled breakdowns can lead to extraordinary breakthroughs.

Declaring a breakdown sends the message, both to one's self and others, that whatever is occurring is no longer acceptable and that new creative action is required. Our consulting experience clearly leads us to the paradoxical conclusion that breakdowns, when handled well, are a major source of breakthroughs. Or said another way: Breakthroughs are typically a well-met series of breakdowns.

To summarize, here is a comparison of the "traditional" way of handling breakdowns versus the "new" way as described in this chapter:

Traditional	**New**
1. Something happens	1. Something happens
2. It occurs as a problem	2. It occurs as a breakdown
3. This shouldn't be! Upset, blame!	3. Declare a breakdown
4. Actions consistent with the upset	4. Actions consistent with the commitment

---

Chapter 8: Key Point to Remember

Notice your human tendency to treat problems and setbacks as things that shouldn't be happening, with the associated finger pointing and upset. Then, treat the breakdown as a normal part of life, and determine and implement actions to resolve the breakdown.

"Vision without action is a daydream."

—— Japanese Proverb

Chapter

Action: The Access to Results

Developing missions, visions or strategies are of little value unless a team can translate them into decisive, coordinated action. This is often referred to as "execution" or "implementation." I prefer the term "action" because it gets to the essence of what generates results. No action, no results.

An average strategy that is well implemented is more valuable than an excellent strategy that is poorly implemented, yet much of corporate America places significantly more effort and emphasis on strategy development than strategy implementation.

Consequently, what we end up with are well-developed strategies that are of limited value. In fact, many strategy documents do little more than take up space on executives' shelves. Missing is the skill to create clear, concise actions on how to achieve the desired strategic priorities.

It's important to recognize that learning the necessary skills to create effective action is critical for success not only in high-level strategic endeavors, but in *all* domains of life and business.

The Action Paradox

The discipline of generating effective action is most powerfully accessed by basic distinctions in our speaking and listening. The paradox here is that actions, which are concrete and *tangible*, are most often the result of effective conversations, which by their nature are *intangible*.

When people train themselves to recognize certain distinctions in speaking and listening, and put these strategies to use, they will experience a true breakthrough in their productivity, as will the people around them. Clear, coordinated action is the pathway to producing the results to which you are committed.

Effective Requests

The most powerful access to the domain of action is a request; although, in reality the requests we make are frequently ineffective. Often, this is because we don't know exactly what it is we want. We fail to do the necessary work to determine our precise intention. Instead of making an effective request, we deliver vague rhetoric, hoping things will somehow turn out okay. It's hard enough to get what we want, but if we don't have a clear idea of what that is, and we don't make an effective request, the results are sure to be disappointing. For the most part, we do not like to accept responsibility for the lack of action. We tend to blame people and circumstances when, in reality, we failed to make a precise, effective request.

Ineffective requests are missing one or more clear conditions of satisfaction – *who* is going to do *what* by *when*. See if you recognize either of these examples of ineffective requesting:

- "Someone needs to work on this report."
- "We need that agenda for the next meeting."

Chances are, you have either made or accepted a request during the past week in which the "who," "what" or "by when" was missing or not clearly stated. One of the reasons meetings are often of limited value is that it is not clear who is being asked to do something, what that something is, and when it is to be completed.

In our workshops we ask clients to assess their own accountability. They figure out where they are stuck, or why something is not moving along with the kind of velocity or progress desired. In helping them resolve their dilemmas, we ask our clients the following:

- "What requests *have* you made?" (Too often, the answer is "very few.")
- "What requests *should* you make?"

The only way to generate action is to make a specific request. If you're not getting the action you desire, you are probably not making those requests. In a nutshell, improved performance requires clear requests.

Committed Responses

However, a request is not effective until you evoke a committed response — a promise, decline or counter-offer. If you have not heard one of these responses, you have not yet communicated for the purpose of action. Therefore, you should not be surprised if no action occurs. In response to a request, people often reply with vague, non-committal answers, "non-promises" in effect. Examples: "I'll try," "I'm working on it," "Don't worry," "I'll take a look at it," "I'll check into it," etc.

In that regard, a key source of effectiveness is *gracious persistence* – graciously persisting until you get a committed response rather than a non-promise. Even the most concise and well-crafted request will be unproductive if it does not evoke a committed response.

I want to emphasize the importance of being willing and able to decline (i.e. to say "No"). If people accept a request out of resignation, compliance or coercion, they cannot authentically say yes! Requests accepted under such conditions undermine vision, commitment, and possibility.

Promises

A promise is a commitment or a guarantee to do something by a certain time with no excuses. A promise says "My word is my bond." This is a fundamental shift in the casual way most of us make promises. All too often we operate under the following formula:

"Results = no results plus a good explanation."

In other words, we say "Yes" publicly, but "No" privately, hoping that an explanation or excuse will forgive the broken vow. In high-performing organizations, when a person says "Yes," it is a commitment you can count on. You can be confident that the task will get done right and on time. When people in an organization can rely on each other in this way, huge productivity gains can occur and unprecedented, measurable results can be achieved.

Applications

In our consulting work, we always devote a section of our workshop to "effective action." The applications of this exercise are almost endless. Nearly all conversations between two or more people will call for action to be taken. This is just as true in a brief, casual conversation in the hallway as it is at a high-level meeting at the United Nations. Our clients role-play conversations, with one person making a targeted request and the other person, through gracious persistence on the requestor's part, offering a committed response. This practice transfers to company meetings with impressive results. In order to be effective, meetings must consist primarily of conversations geared toward action, with all promises recorded on an *action register*. This can be as simple as a flipchart with each desired action illustrated on a page with three columns: Who, What, When. We have found that using these action registers is far more effective than the traditional recording of meeting minutes.

Summary

Let's summarize the requirements for action-oriented conversations:

When you make a **promise** to do something, state exactly *what* you will do by *when*.

When you **request** something from someone, state your intentions clearly and concisely. A request must include all three of the following elements: *what* (specifically), *to whom*, and *when by*.

For each request, obtain a **committed response**. A committed response is one of the following: *accept/promise* ("yes"), *decline* ("no"), or *counter offer*.

Guidelines:

- Effectiveness is being able to get a clear committed response. Practice "gracious persistence." Don't give up too soon.

- Remember, clear commitments are anchored in time.
- Put it in writing! This keeps the promise in view and enhances clarity.
- Complaints can often be converted to requests.
- Enrollment is aided by speaking to the impact of the action — the benefits of taking the action.

Conclusion

Conversations that produce action consist of effective promises, requests and committed responses. These are the language acts that access the domain of action. If we are not making effective promises and requests and evoking committed responses, action is unlikely to occur.

I propose that we expand the role of management to include the management of conversations, so that we speak in a way that is intentional and action-oriented. The best leaders make big requests and big promises. In addition, they are compassionate and grateful; they know what they are asking for and they understand the effort it takes for someone to deliver the desired action. Clearly, leadership requires an understanding of how to communicate for action. When done right, this communication will generate enormous results.

✳✳✳

Chapter 9: Key Point to Remember

Always remember the results you produce are a function of the actions you take. Effective actions are determined by your rigor in stating requests and promises, and for each request and promise, specifying who is going to do what by when.

"Think like a wise man,
but communicate in the language of the people."

—— William Butler Yeats

Chapter

Life (and Work) is a Conversation

Most people don't realize the extent to which conversation shapes our world. All meaningful interaction occurs through language. In Chapter 2 we learned about the benefits of effective listening. In this chapter, we will explore the other side of conversation — speaking. We'll discover ways to use our speech for maximum effectiveness and satisfaction. The power to design the future success of an endeavor, in life or in business, resides in our ability to structure conversation.

While working with a major food manufacturer, we were able to solve a problem between their R&D and marketing departments simply by altering their language patterns. We helped them shift their conversation from we/they and turf issues to a language of collaboration and shared vision. Once they replaced their long-held tendency to compete with each other and prove each other wrong, the two departments proclaimed trust in each other and made a joint commitment to introduce a new product. By creating a mutually supportive relationship, the new product was successfully introduced in two years rather than the traditional four years, and added millions of dollars to their bottom line, creating a strategic advantage over their competition.

Over the course of our work with many different organizations in this area, we have identified three styles of speaking that have yielded positive results for our clients. For our purposes here the term "conversation" refers not just to speech, but also to certain non-verbal communications, including policies, procedures, plans, reports and e-mails. For example, when a company issues a policy statement to their employees, this statement must be read and responded to, either through actions or words. This, in effect, constitutes conversations. If our success depends on effective conversations, we must learn to become proficient at speaking and listening.

The three types of speaking in which we encourage proficiency in order to improve interactions and, consequently, effectiveness include: Straight Talk, Alignment and Acknowledgment.

Straight Talk

Straight talk is the type of full-disclosure conversation that results in action and improvement. As the name suggests, straight talk is straightforward, sincere, open and honest. Think of it as bringing "hallway" conversation into the room. Straight talk can be either positive or negative, but it is not a license to damage another or stop an action.

When done right, straight talk should result in a situation where people are actively and mutually supporting each other's success by honestly communicating about what's working and what is not.

We all have blind spots. It's been said that human beings see out of the wrong side of their eyes; that is, we see what is wrong with others, but we have difficulty seeing those same flaws in ourselves. One of the best ways to improve what isn't working or strengthen those things that are working is to provide straight talk to others and be open to receiving straight talk in return.

Straight talk is the foundation of high performance. It supports our own growth and the growth of the people with whom we interact. It is an essential skill for any high-performance leader, team or organization.

Alignment

High performance also requires *alignment* — the willingness to authentically support a decision or course of action, whether one agrees with it or not. Alignment does not necessarily imply agreement.

Managers often confuse consensus or agreement with

Tips for Providing Straight Talk:

- State what's observable (facts, not opinions).
- Example: "You interrupted me three times during today's meeting," versus "You are rude."
- Example: "I appreciate the extra help you gave Joe yesterday," versus "You are a real team player."
- Speak to the person, not to a third party.
- Example: "You were late for the meeting — that didn't work for me," versus complaining to somebody else.
- Look person straight in the eye — use first person.
- Don't delay — it festers.
- If you feel uncomfortable, it's okay. Straight talk takes practice.
- If in doubt, say it.

Tips on Receiving Straight Talk:

- Try it on — don't be defensive.
- Listen to feedback not necessarily as the truth, but as a valid point of view, a valid perspective.
- Say one thing only, "Thank You."

alignment. Consensus is one of several decision-making processes (including majority rule, authority rule, etc.), while alignment represents the relationship one has to a decision.

One can own and fully support the decision without necessarily agreeing with it.

The most important issue is not the process with which a decision is reached; rather, it is whether those involved are willing to genuinely support and fulfill the decision. This is alignment. Regardless of your role in making the decision, and regardless of whether you actually agree with the decision that was made, it is still possible for you to align with a decision.

This does not mean rolling over and giving up. You need not surrender your voice in order to align. Alignment allows you to clearly state your views, but requires that you be willing to take ownership in, abide by, and be accountable for decisions that represent a different point of view. Alignment empowers a decision and increases the likelihood that the decision will lead to the desired result. In the end, workability is more important than having the same views. Alignment may involve giving up the right to be right, or to win the argument.

People who are aligned realize that the ownership and support of a decision may have more to do with success than the quality of the decision.

What creates alignment is actually very different from what creates compliance. Most people mistakenly try to get others to agree on a course of action. Yet it is difficult to get two people to agree on what to have for lunch, let alone trying to get 500 people to agree on a corporate strategy! On a football team, the wide receiver does not refuse to block merely because he thinks the coach should have called a pass play instead of a running play; rather, he aligns with the decision and proceeds with the play as though it was his call.

Alignment is the individual's self-generated identification with the purpose of the group, because the purpose of the group is seen as larger than one's own objectives.

Acknowledgment

Acknowledgment is the authentic expression of appreciation for another person. We are often unaware of what makes us ineffective, and even more unaware of what makes us effective! Unless others acknowledge us and we allow ourselves to hear it, we cannot build on our strengths.

Acknowledgment is authentic. It is not saying something simply to make another feel good.

Acknowledgment is not saying something to make a person like us or agree with us. Instead, acknowledgment provides people with the knowledge and understanding that they do, in fact, make a difference and that they are truly appreciated. Acknowledgment enhances team relationships and results, and adds greatly to an individual's capacity to take initiative.

While most people are truly aware of the importance of

Examples of barriers to giving (speaking) acknowledgment:

"Bob already knows what a good job he did."

"She is paid to do that anyway."

"He will feel like I expect something in return."

"It will look like favoritism."

"It will be embarrassing."

Examples of barriers to receiving (hearing) acknowledgment:

"It's just my job."

"I wonder what he wants in return for this acknowledgment."

"I'm embarrassed."

"He doesn't really mean it."

"It was really no big deal."

acknowledgement, there are barriers to both giving and receiving acknowledgment. [See examples on page 65.]

As a result of these barriers, relatively few people experience the satisfaction that comes from offering or receiving authentic acknowledgment.

In order for acknowledgment to occur, people need to be consciously aware of the contributions and accomplishments of others and give themselves permission to express their appreciation.

If the recipient deflects the acknowledgment or doesn't seem to fully hear it, the speaker must work harder to make himself heard. This may mean looking the person directly in the eye and saying: "Stop for a moment. I want to make sure you really heard what I said."

We have found that high-performing organizations are filled with people who authentically express appreciation for one another. It is part of the everyday culture of the organization.

The most powerful tools we have at our disposal to direct the outcome of our endeavors is the ability to converse efficiently and effectively. Straight Talk, Alignment and Acknowledgement are three techniques that have helped our clients reach their peak performance levels.

※※※

Chapter 10: Key Point to Remember

As human beings we can say that life (and work) is truly a series of conversations. Some of our conversations actually make a difference, some do not. Conversations that make a difference include straight talk, alignment and acknowledgment.

"Commitment is what transforms a promise into reality. It is the words that speak boldly of your stand, and the actions which speak louder than words. Commitment is the stuff character is made of; the power to change the face of things, to create a new future."

—— Anonymous

11
Chapter

Conclusion — The Three Domains of Life and Business

Someone once said "all models are wrong; some are useful." Underlying each of the chapters in this book is a model I have used in my consulting work. I call it the "Three Domain" model. I offer it to you with the hope that you will find it useful.

The purpose of the Three Domain model is to help you *choose* the type of thinking and behaviors that will guide your actions, resulting in maximum effectiveness.

The model is quite simple — three circles in a row, each representing one of life's domains: Past, Present and Future. The assumption is that our present actions can be influenced by either our memories of past experiences (left circle) or our vision of the future (right circle). As the diagram shows, past influences include such things as our previous judgments, assessments, interpretations or explanations. If we let the future affect our present actions, we are guided by different influences: Commitment; Possibility; Vision; Mission. Every person must ultimately choose which domain will most often guide their actions.

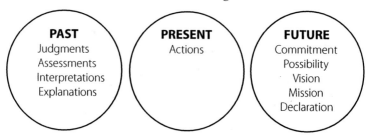

I have found that effective people choose more of their actions based on future influences. Unfortunately, most people are more impacted by factors from the past. In our workshops, we ask participants to estimate what percentage of their time they spend in each of the three domains. Their answers are quite revealing: on average, they reported that they typically spend between 40-50% in the past domain, 40-50% in the present domain and almost *no* time in the future domain.

I would argue that each of us would benefit from rebalancing the time and energy we spend in each of the two outside domains. In many ways, the purpose of this book is to motivate people to have more of their actions guided by future influences than by the past judgments and assumptions that currently drive most of their actions.

If you look back at some of the stories within the past chapters, you will find many examples of how the "Three Domain" model was the underlying driving force behind many of the breakthrough actions.

In Chapter 2 — **The Gift of Listening** — I described our human tendency to engage in "automatic" listening. You will recall that this type of listening is based on our pre-conceived judgments (the left circle). We also learned that we can choose to engage in creative listening, which is more generous and "other" focused. When we do this, we are essentially creating a new future with that person — one that is defined by who the person really is. This is right circle thinking: it is future-oriented.

In Chapter 3 — **Angels in Disguise** — we acknowledged our propensity to discredit people who look or act differently. By making this hasty assessment, we allow past influences to dictate our present action. When we choose to treat others with dignity and respect, we are letting future possibilities dictate our actions.

In Chapter 4 — **The 100/0 Principle** — I discussed the common denominator of most relationships, which is where we determine the relationship with another person based on whether we agree with them or not. The right circle version of this decision is taking 100% responsibility — fully committing ourselves — to the important relationships in our lives.

In Chapter 5 — **Put Self on the Shelf** — you may recall the story of David Neeleman, former CEO of JetBlue Airways. When he made the decision to go to the slums of Brazil to help the poor, no doubt his left circle (past influences) literally screamed at him not to go. But with an eye toward the future he went anyway, and he would be the first to remind us what a life-altering experience that was for him.

In Chapter 6 — **Ashley is a Blessing** — I introduced you to my daughters Ashley and Andrea. When Ashley was born, medical professionals advised my wife and me to institutionalize her. Why? Because children like Ashley "are always a burden to other family members." While I'm certain these professionals meant well, this is classic left-circle thinking. They were asking us to allow *their* past experiences to guide *our* action with our daughter.

Thankfully, with guidance from other parents of disabled children, God's grace and our fundamental commitment to our daughter, we decided to bring Ashley home and create a future together. Had we not allowed our actions to be dictated by a future commitment, we would have robbed ourselves, and countless others, of the blessing of knowing Ashley and receiving her unconditional love.

In Chapter 7 — **The Little Stuff is the Big Stuff** — we witnessed how forgiving those who have hurt us in the past allows us to move into the future with grace and peace.

In Chapter 8 — **Breakdowns can Produce Breakthroughs** — we saw several examples of people who actually used setbacks to accelerate their progress toward their goals. When a breakdown occurs, our natural tendency is to go immediately to the left circle, saying things like: "I knew something like this would happen," or "I knew we couldn't count on him/her/them." In other words, we try to explain why the breakdown happened, who was at fault, and worse — why we can't move forward. When operating out of the right circle, however, we renew our commitment to the goal and set our sights on creating something new. This helps us resolve the breakdown in a powerful way that actually leads us to an eventual breakthrough.

One word of caution about the Three Domain model: I am not suggesting that all our actions should be driven by the right circle. Think about it — it would be folly for us to forget about that left circle (Past). The left circle informs us to stop on red and go on green. It reminds us to thoughtfully assess a situation before acting. I am simply suggesting that it would be wise to allow many *more* of our actions to be influenced by right circle components.

The Power of the Future Domain

I cannot overemphasize the power of the right circle. The components of this circle are the "stuff" that success is made of:

- Commitments/Promises
- Visions
- Missions
- Strategies
- One's "stand" on issues

When we let these components guide our actions, the results are extraordinary:

- Creativity
- Innovation
- Unprecedented results
- BREAKTHROUGHS!

The right circle is about making a commitment, or "taking a stand." It's about recognizing that preconceived notions, opinions, and judgments are insufficient. It's about recognizing the strong tendency to drift to the left circle and allow our actions to be guided by past experiences. When we consciously move to the future domain, we interrupt the past influence. This requires that we become aware and intentional. It demands that we take 100% responsibility for outcomes and relationships. It forces us to stop letting our feelings, moods or discomfort block our path to our success.

If you take just one concept from this book, let it be this: You are each capable of choosing behaviors that go against the "drift." You each have the prerogative of choosing the behaviors, many of which are found in the pages of this book, that are counter-intuitive or paradoxical in nature. I trust you will find that by consciously choosing the "road less traveled," you will vastly improve your effectiveness, experience greater personal satisfaction and achieve breakthrough results in your personal and business life.

⁂⁂⁂

Chapter 11: Key Point to Remember

Always recognize your human tendency to "drift" to the left (the past) circle, then consciously and deliberately dwell in the right (the future) circle so that more of your current actions (the present) are driven by the future you are creating rather than your past assessments and judgments.

Personal and Professional Effectiveness Exercises

On the following pages, you will find exercises that will help you apply the concepts in this book to your life. Follow the steps and practice the exercises either alone or in a group. You will be surprised at how easily these skills transfer to your daily life.

CHAPTER 1: SLOW DOWN IN ORDER TO SPEED UP

Exercise: Implementation of Slow-Down Techniques

Purpose of Exercise: To help you identify and commit to ways to slow down or cease your daily activities in order to increase focus and productivity.

Time Required: 30 minutes if done alone, more time if done with others.

Instructions: Figure out some areas where you can slow down or cease activities during your day. Be creative and precise. Any and all ideas, even seemingly crazy ones, are appropriate.

- List those ideas on a flip chart, chalkboard or paper.
- Clarify the meaning of those ideas that need clarification.
- Argue for the ideas that look feasible.
- Select two or three of the ideas and commit to implementing them.
- Determine what actions you will take to implement the ideas.

If others are involved in the exercise, align on how to hold each other accountable for these actions.

CHAPTER 2: THE GIFT OF LISTENING

Exercise #1: Revealing your Automatic Listening

Purpose of Exercise: To identify the underlying attitudes and preconceived notions that affect the way you listen to others.

Time Required: 10 minutes

Instructions: Take out a pen or pencil and write down the first word or phrase that comes to your mind when you see each of the following words or names. Don't over-think this:

- George Bush
- Barry Bonds
- Hillary Clinton
- Meetings
- Consultants
- Iraq
- China
- Abortion
- McDonalds
- Global Warming

Your rapid first responses will reflect the attitudes you carry with you. These attitudes will affect the way you hear things that others say.

Exercise #2: Shifting Your Listening

Purpose of Exercise: To help you identify your patterns of "automatic listening," the consequences of that form of listening, and ways to generate a more effective listening style.

Time Required: 10 minutes if done alone, or one hour if done in a team setting, where you and others write out the answers, then share those answers with each other.

Instructions: Think of a person about whom you have a negative judgment and do the following:

- Identify the way in which you listen "automatically" to what this person has to say.
- Notice how this automatic listening influences your behavior with this person.
- Determine a new (creative) way to listen to this person. How would this new form of listening affect your interactions with this person?
- Determine what you and the other person would gain from your new form of listening.

Exercise #3: Practicing Creative Listening

Purpose of Exercise: To help you develop and practice a new and more effective listening style.

Time Required: 10 minutes if done alone, or one hour if done in a team setting, with each team member sharing their responses.

Instructions: Recall a situation in which you received feedback.

- How would you describe your "automatic listening" to the person giving the feedback?
- How could you have incorporated "creative listening" into that situation? In other words, what could you have listened for?
- If you had been able to listen creatively, what questions would you have asked the person giving you the feedback?
- How would your feelings have changed about the feedback?
- What alternative views, interpretations, or actions might have resulted?

CHAPTER 3: ANGELS IN DISGUISE

Exercise: Searching for an Angel

Purpose of Exercise: To provide you with greater access to "angels" in your life.

Time Required: 15 minutes

Instructions: List people you have avoided because they look or act differently or are from a different background, social or economic position than you.

Select one of these people and commit to initiating a conversation with him/her by a specified date.

If others are involved in the exercise, make promises to each other and align on how you will hold each other accountable.

CHAPTER 4: THE 100/0 PRINCIPLE

Exercise: Taking Responsibility for a Relationship

Purpose of Exercise: To practice taking responsibility for the success of a relationship.

Time Required: 10 minutes if done alone, or one hour in a team setting where you and others write out your answers, then share with teammates.

Instructions: Think of a relationship in which you are not fully satisfied (for example, an individual from whom you are not getting the level of cooperation you would like).

- Figure out if you are trying to be "right" about something, and if so, what?

- Are you indeed right about this issue? What are others telling you about how right you are?

- Decide if you are more interested in making the relationship work or in being right.

- If you decide that the relationship is more important, decide what actions you will take to improve the relationship and by when.

CHAPTER 5: PUT SELF ON THE SHELF

Exercise: Shifting from Entitlement to Servitude

Purpose of Exercise: To give you practice in consciously placing attention on another rather than on yourself.

Time Required: 20 minutes or longer if others are involved.

Instructions: Recall a past event where you served another without being required to do so.

- How did that make the other person feel? How did that make you feel?
- Were there any unexpected positive results that came from serving that person?
- Who in your present life can you serve in some way, big or small?
- Decide what you will do for that person and by when.

CHAPTER 6: ASHLEY IS A BLESSING

Exercise: Breaking Through Your Discomfort

Purpose of Exercise: To take the first steps to overcoming your discomfort with people who are mentally or physically challenged.

Time Required: 10 minutes or longer if it is a team activity.

Instructions: If you come across someone in the next week who has a disability, make it a point to simply say "hello," then:

- Observe that person's response. If it is appropriate, add something more to the conversation, such as "How are you doing?" or "Where are you from?"
- Notice what happens; you will be pleasantly surprised.
- Continue to do this week after week when you come across people with disabilities. You will be amazed at how quickly your discomfort will disappear. In other words, you will be blessed.

CHAPTER 7: THE LITTLE STUFF IS THE BIG STUFF

Exercise: Doing a Little Thing Well

Purpose of Exercise: To help you create a breakthrough by focusing on a little thing.

Time Required: 20 minutes or longer if others are involved.

Instructions: Review Chapter 7 to remind you of some of the little things that can make a big difference.

- Choose one of these things and make a promise to implement it each day for the next week.
- In a team setting, decide how you will hold each other accountable to do this.

CHAPTER 8: BREAKDOWNS CAN PRODUCE BREAKTHROUGHS

Exercise: Coaching a Person with a Breakdown

Purpose of Exercise: To help you effectively handle a breakdown; to give you practice in coaching others on handling a breakdown.

Time Required: 20 minutes if done alone, 30 to 90 minutes if two or more people are involved.

Instructions: In a small group (2-3 people), each person takes a turn describing an actual breakdown they have experienced. The others coach the person through the exercise to create a breakthrough. The coaches avoid the temptation to provide answers. Rather, help the person create new solutions by asking questions.

- Declare the breakdown.
- Distinguish facts from emotions.
- Regenerate the commitment.
    - What is the commitment that makes these facts a breakdown?
- Given that commitment, what do you see as possible actions?
    - Brainstorm possible actions.
- To which possible actions are you committed?
- What actions will you take?
    - Requests and promises (who, what and when).

CHAPTER 9: ACTION—THE ACCESS TO RESULTS

Exercise: Getting Into Effective Action

Purpose of Exercise: To help you design actions to achieve a real set of priorities.

Time Required: 30 minutes if working alone, 90 minutes in a team setting.

Instructions: It's important that you:

- Review your priorities or goals
- Design an action plan, including:
  - Initiatives (what you promise to do, and by when)
  - Requests (what you want others to do, and by when)
- If in a team setting, report on your action plan, and manage conversations for:
  - Getting a committed response (yes, no or counter-offer) to your requests
  - Alignment regarding your initiatives

Example: Our goal is to be the #1 supplier of widgets in the world.

Initiative: I will perform a research study on all widget manufacturers in the world, showing the industry and each manufacturer, growth rates, time in business, strengths and weaknesses, opportunities and threats, strategic priorities, sales and earnings history and projections. This research will be completed and distributed to each of the widget team members by (month, day, year).

Ask the team: "Are you aligned on this action?" If they all say "yes," great. If one or more say "no," ask what will it take for them to be aligned? Then make any changes to the action until all team members fully support the action.

Request: I request Joe Smith and Julie Jones to be available any two days a week to assist me on the research study. Graciously persist until Joe and Julie say "yes," "no" or state a counter offer.

CHAPTER 10: LIFE (AND WORK) IS A CONVERSATION

Exercise: Feedback Exercise

Purpose of Exercise: To get team-based practice in giving and receiving feedback.

Time Required: 2 hours for a team of six to eight people.

Instructions: This exercise provides an opportunity to take powerful steps toward becoming a great team. Each team member will give and receive feedback from the others using Straight Talk as the guiding principle. We all have blind spots regarding what is working and what is not. The best path to corrective action is by receiving constructive feedback, both positive and negative, by teammates.

- Each person reviews the principles of Straight Talk in Chapter 10.

- Each person prepares a sheet of paper for each teammate, by writing the name of each teammate on the top of a sheet of paper. Then write three column headings: Increase, Decrease, Retain on each sheet.

- Each person writes, in observable terms in each column, the feedback to offer each of the other people, using the principles of straight talk. Each person takes about 30 minutes to fill out the sheets. Possible areas for feedback: leadership, follow-through, team player, communication, listening skills, willingness to be coached, handling of breakdowns, risk-taking, creativity, etc. Be specific regarding observable behavior. Be brief — maximum two bullets per column. If in doubt about whether to include something, include it.

In the verbal feedback, adhere to feedback guidelines:

- Speak in the first person.

- Look person in the eye.

- When giving feedback, be specific. When receiving feedback, acknowledge your assessor's ideas as valid. Try on the advice. If it works for you, fine. If not ... that's fine too!

- Each participant must go under the "spotlight," where they listen to each person's feedback. One person takes notes for the one be-ing spotlighted. *(This usually is uncomfortable at first, but you'd be surprised at how quickly the discomfort dissipates.)*

- Each person writes down at least one promise and one request based on the feedback they received. Each person then states their promise(s), makes their request(s) and obtains committed responses.

- Discuss ways to maintain the promises and requests.

- People share their feelings about the exercise.

ABOUT THE AUTHOR

Al Ritter has an MBA from the Amos Tuck School at Dartmouth College and has spent the last 20 years as a management consultant. Before becoming a consultant, he held senior level positions with Citicorp, PepsiCo and Swift & Company.

Al is a sought-after expert in leadership development, building high performance teams, strategy planning and implementation, managing large scale change, and strengthening corporate culture. His consulting clients span numerous industries, both in the United States and abroad. He is a frequent speaker for businesses and professional groups, and conducts numerous seminars and workshops.

An accomplished athlete, Al played basketball and baseball for the University of Connecticut and currently participates in triathlons. He sits on the board of several non-profit organizations in the Chicago area.

CONTRIBUTOR (Chapter 6)

Andrea Ritter is Al's daughter and a 2006 graduate of Hope College in Holland, Michigan with a teaching degree in special education. She is an elementary school teacher in Aurora, Illinois. Andrea's experience with her sister and other special needs people is a powerful testimony to the paradox that so-called "normal" people can often learn more from "special" people than vice versa.

HOW TO REACH US

Al Ritter's firm, The Ritter Consulting Group, is an internationally recognized coaching and consulting firm, dedicated to helping leaders, teams and organizations deliver breakthrough performance.

For inquiries about speaking engagements, executive and team development, cultural change, large-scale change management, or strategy development and implementation, please call 630.673.4254; email ahritter7@aol.com, or go to our website at www.ritterconsultinggroup. com, which provides more information about the specific services we provide and benefits our clients realize.